BERKLEE BASIC GUITAR

WILLIAM LEAVITT

PHASE 1

Berklee Press

Director: Dave Kusek
Managing Editor: Debbie Cavalier
Marketing Manager: Ola Frank
Sr. Writer/Editor: Jonathan Feist

ISBN 978-0-6340-1333-1

berklee press

1140 Boylston Street
Boston, MA 02215-3693 USA
(617) 747-2146

Visit Berklee Press Online at
www.berkleepress.com

DISTRIBUTED BY

HAL•LEONARD®
CORPORATION
7777 W. BLUEMOUND RD. P.O. BOX 13819
MILWAUKEE, WISCONSIN 53213

Visit Hal Leonard Online at
www.halleonard.com

INTRODUCTION

PURPOSE:

Why was this book written?. . . . TO PROVIDE FUN while learning to speak the language of music through one of the oldest instruments in existence. The antiquity of the guitar and its continuing popularity certainly indicates that countless numbers of people have enjoyed performing on, and listening to it down through the centuries. The guitar (you will discover) has the peculiar ability to charm and please when played at any musical level, from very elemental to highly complex.

Also this book is to acquaint the student with the guitar as a complete musical instrument, with solo and orchestral potential in addition to its more well known capability for the accompaniment of others.

METHOD:

How is this to be accomplished? The lesson material is set up so that there is a GRADUAL PHYSICAL DEVELOPMENT of strength and co-ordination of the hands as well as a beginning AWARENESS OF THE WORKINGS OF MUSIC itself. Therefore this book is not just about the guitar but also about music.

The two, three and four part arrangements (are designed to) provide fun through musically interesting material for class instruction, guitar clubs and student recitals.

So good luck, and enjoy yourself. . . .

Wm. G. Leavitt

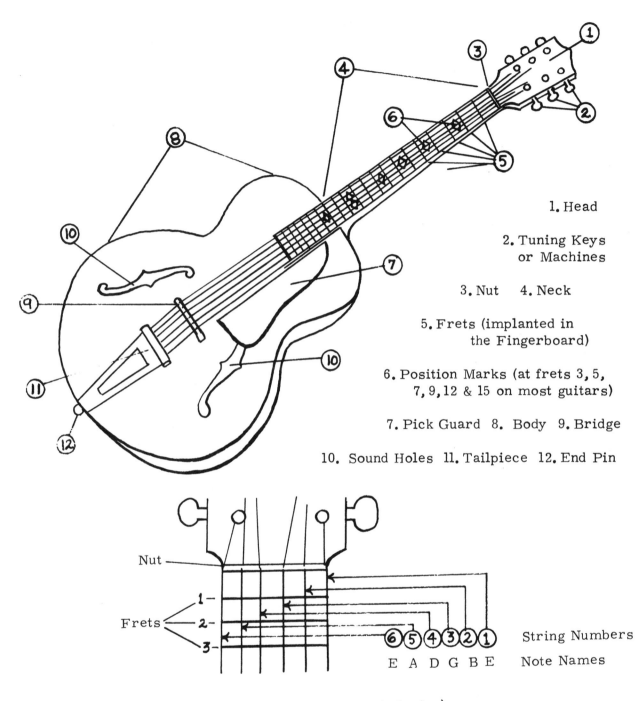

1. Head

2. Tuning Keys or Machines

3. Nut   4. Neck

5. Frets (implanted in the Fingerboard)

6. Position Marks (at frets 3, 5, 7, 9, 12 & 15 on most guitars)

7. Pick Guard   8. Body   9. Bridge

10. Sound Holes   11. Tailpiece   12. End Pin

Nut

Frets

String Numbers					
6	5	4	3	2	1
E	A	D	G	B	E

String Numbers

Note Names

TO TUNE THE GUITAR: (using piano or pitch pipe)

1. Tune the open 1st string to the first E above middle C...
2. Press the 2nd string down at the fifth fret and tune (2nd stg.) until it sounds exactly the same as the open 1st string......
3. Press the 3rd string down at the fourth fret and tune (3rd stg.) until it sounds exactly the same as the open 2nd string...
4. Press 4th string at fifth fret... tune to open 3rd string.....
5. " 5th " " " " ... " " " 4th " ....
6. " 6th " " " " ... " " " 5th " .....

1

POSTURES

THE LEFT HAND

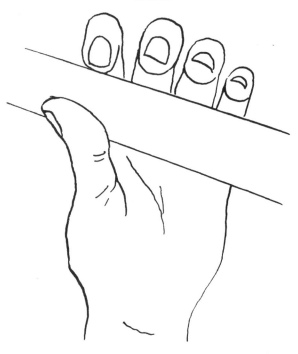

The palm must never hug the neck..
The thumb remains on the back of
the neck just above center

THE RIGHT HAND

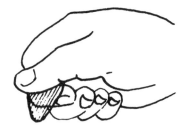

The pick is held between the
bent 1st finger and thumb

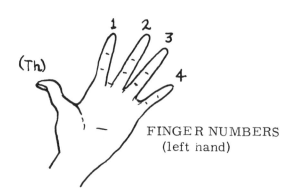

FINGER NUMBERS
(left hand)

THE STAFF: consists of 5 lines and 4 spaces, and is divided into MEASURES by BAR LINES.....

bar   bar   double
line   line   bar line

CLEF SIGN: Guitar music is written in the TREBLE (or "G") clef, and the number of sharps (#) or flats (♭) found next to the clef sign indicate the KEY SIGNATURE. (to be explained more fully at a later time...)

 "G" clef shows the position of the note G

"COMMON" TIME VALUES OF THE NOTES:

whole note   half notes   quarter notes   eighth notes (in groups).....(or singlely)

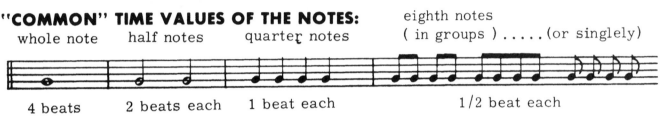

4 beats   2 beats each   1 beat each   1/2 beat each

TIME SIGNATURES: Next to the clef sign (at the beginning of a composition) are found two numbers (like a fraction) or a symbol which represents these numbers. The top number tells how many beats (or counts) in a measure, and the bottom number indicates what kind of note gets one beat.

EXAMPLE: $\frac{4}{4}$ means four quarters, or four beats per measure with a quarter note receiving one beat, or count. The symbol is... **C**

The musical alphabet consists of the first seven letters of the alphabet for language. Going up the scale the note names progress up the alphabet...A B C D E F.G, A B C D etc....
....Going down the scale the note names progress down the alphabet (like reading it backwards)...G F E D C B A, G F E D etc...

THE LEFT HAND

The 1st finger will play only the notes that fall on the 1st fret..
The 2nd finger " " " " " " " " the 2nd fret..
The 3rd finger " " " " " " " " the 3rd fret..
The 4th finger " " " " " " " " the 4th fret..

AN OPEN STRING is not touched by the left hand. The proper
note is produced by merely picking the string.

THE THUMB is not used to produce any notes and should remain
on the back of the neck slightly above center.

> Press the string down sharply and firmly just behind the fret...
> ...If you get a buzzing sound you must press more quickly, or
> with more pressure, or closer to the fret.

THE G CLEF shows where the note G is located on the staff   The 3rd string of the guitar is tuned to this note.

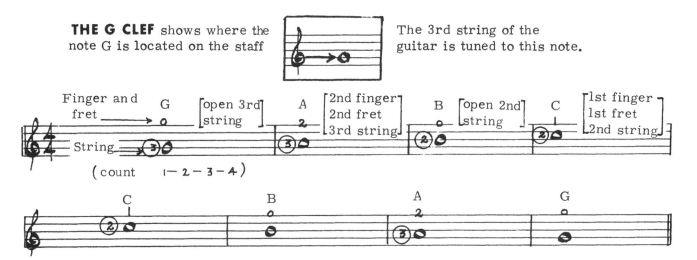

Half Note-Whole Note Studies

1.

4

2.

(1 – 2   3 – 4)   (1 – 2 – 3 – 4)

3.

READ THE NOTES... NOT the fingering, as these numbers
will not always be there to help you....

4.

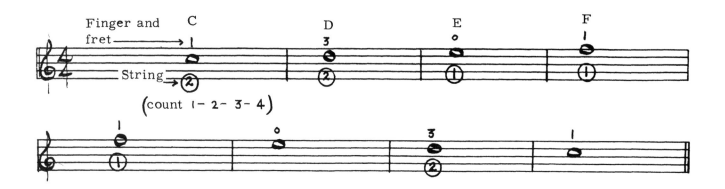

Half Note -Whole Note Studies

5.

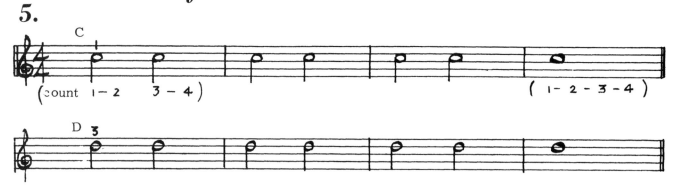

6.

7.

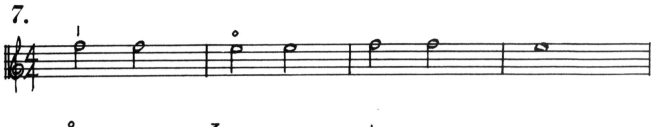

Try not to look at your hands, and you will be surprised at
how quickly they will learn to judge the distances.

8.

Press the strings down quickly and firmly...Avoid the buzz.

REGULAR REVIEW of all previous lesson material is a must! Always
practice, playing at an even tempo (speed). Tapping the foot is often
a big help. Slow, steady practice and constant review of ALL preceding
studies guarantees improvement.

A note with the same sound and letter name but twice as high (or low) in pitch is called an OCTAVE...

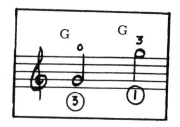

First Duet

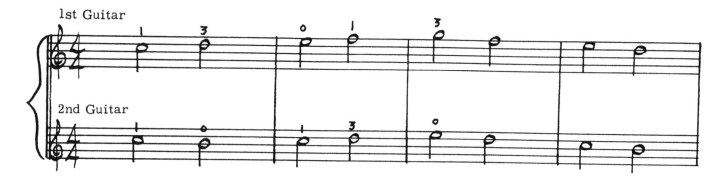

Half Note - Whole Note Duet

8

(The student must learn all parts of all arrangements)

ASSIGNMENT . . . . Write the letter names over the following notes. . . . . . Play. . . .

FIRST CHORDS

* Strum = Push the pick very quickly across the strings. . . be careful
to strum only those strings necessary for the chord.

9

TIME SIGNATURE ... Top number tells how many beats per measure ...

Bottom number tells what kind of note gets one beat...

Quarter Notes In Four, Four Time

1st

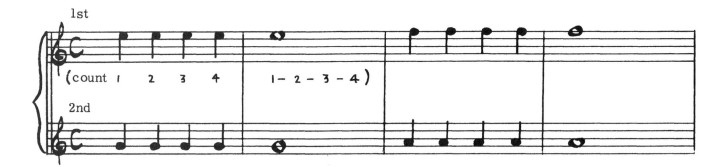

(count 1   2   3   4   1 – 2 – 3 – 4)

2nd

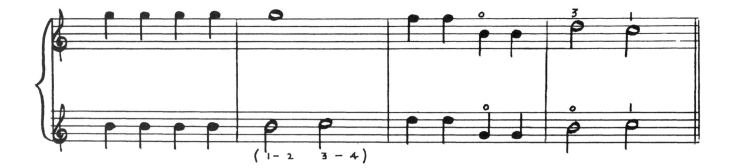

(1 – 2   3 – 4)

THE WHOLE NOTE REST

A "REST" is a period of silence, or a silent note.

OBSERVE:... The Whole Rest "hangs below" the 4th line of the staff.

1st

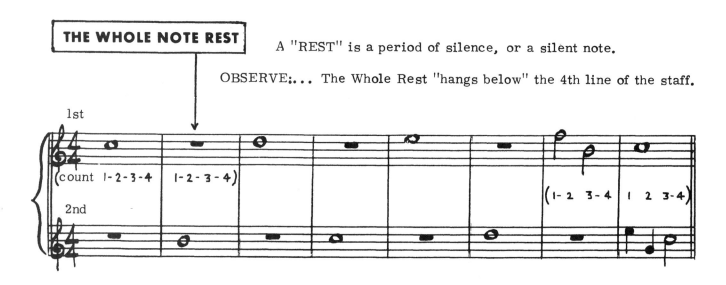

(count 1-2-3-4   1-2-3-4)   (1-2 3 – 4   1   2   3-4)

2nd

The Count

W.G.L.

THE HALF NOTE REST

OBSERVE.. The Half Rest "sits on" the 3rd line of the staff

ASSIGNMENT . . . . . . .Write note names and insert barlines.. (observe time Signature). Play..

11

The Count Returns

W.G.L.

THE QUARTER NOTE REST

(count 1 2 3 4)

12

Old Mac

* These are called REHEARSAL NUMBERS. They are a great help to all when you must practice certain sections of an arrangement. Everyone can quickly find the first measure of the section that needs more work.

** Do not allow open strings to ring through a rest... Silence them by lightly touching with the side (fleshy part) of the right hand palm.

Note: All three part arrangements are playable as duets.. the 3rd guitar part is always optional and may be omitted.)

QUARTER NOTES IN THREE, FOUR TIME

count 1 2 3   1 2 3   1 - 2 3   1 2 - 3

The Waltz

W. G. L.

1st

2nd

Ritard (Get Slower)

ASSIGNMENT . . . . Write note names and insert bar lines . . (Observe time signature) . . Play

CHORD SYMBOLS AND DIAGRAMS

All CHORD SYMBOLS (names) appearing only as a letter are assumed to be MAJOR chords. A letter followed by the numeral "7" represents a DOMINANT 7th chord. A letter followed by a small "m" (or sometimes a dash (-) is a MINOR chord.

A CHORD DIAGRAM is actually a picture of the guitar fingerboard. The vertical lines are the strings and the horizontal lines are the frets. The black dots show finger placement. Numbers found below the diagram indicate which fingers are to be used. A zero(O)represents an open string. Be careful to strike only tne strings indicated for the chord.

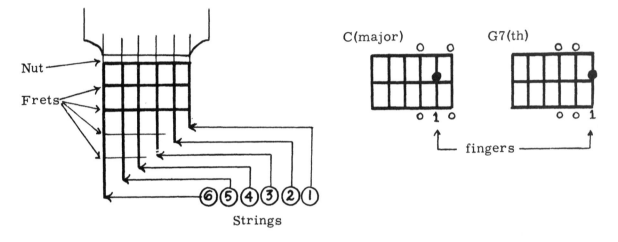

Note: Tne TOP STRINGS are the ones with the highest sound... The BOTTOM STRINGS nave the lowest sound... This is sometimes confusing as it is just the reverse of their physical position when the guitar is on your lap.

Also note: As you know when playing single string (one note at a time) the 4 fingers of the left hand are assigned to the frets with the same numbers. (1st finger - 1st fret, 2nd finger - 2nd fret, etc.)
When playing cnords we must often break this rule to form the chords.

... Being aware of the beginner's impatience to play more chords, I have included, at the back of the book, chord diagrams of the more important open or 1st position chords. It will do no harm whatsoever if you sneak back there and go at them anytime from here on... providing that you observe the fingerings and... of course do not slight your regular lesson material...

Theme From The Surprise Symphony

J. Haydn

* Pronounced "Fee-Nay"....It means - The End

Big Ben

(The 1st guitar part is primarily designed to strengthen the 1st finger)

W.G.L.

* Both the 1st and 2nd strings are to be pressed down by the 1st finger (1st fret).

The following new notes are an OCTAVE below those learned on Page 6

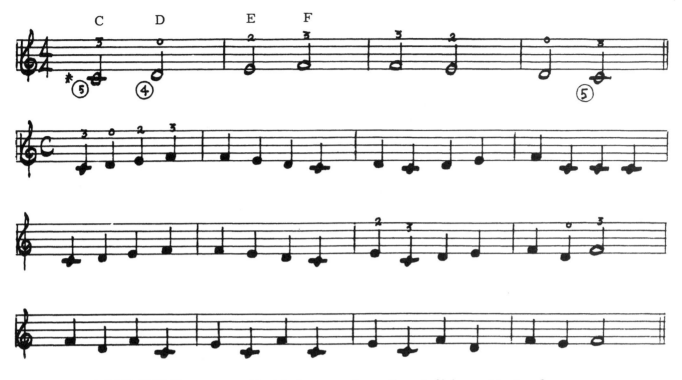

* LEDGER lines are added below or above the staff for notes too low
or too high to appear on the staff.....

CHORD STUDY

The following chords are played on the 2nd, 3rd, and 4th
strings. Avoid playing the 1st string by pushing the pick
up against it...using it as a pick stop.

keep fingers pressed down——let notes ring

19

Another Waltz

Introducing the "TIE"... when two notes are tied together with a curved line,
only the first note is picked... the second note is just held and counted.

* Do not allow any open strings to ring through a rest... silence them by
touching with the side (fleshy part) of the right hand.

THE C MAJOR SCALE ....one octave from C to C

The C Major Scale is made up of all "natural" notes.. (no sharps or flats).
MEMORIZE THIS.... All natural notes are a whole step apart except E to F
and B to C - they are the only natural half steps....

ASSIGNMENT ....Write note names and insert bar lines... (Observe time Signature)..Play

20

TIED NOTES AND DOTTED HALF NOTES
(The following is a comparison of notation -not a duet)

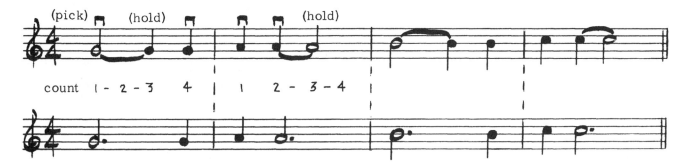

(A "dot" placed after any note increases the time value of the note by one half.)

Duet For Dot

W.G.L.

(*Dm means D Minor)

White Coral Bells

(* ROUND)

2nd Gtr(s) "TACET"... remain silent..(4 measures)

* ROUND = A repetitious melody so constructed that it can be played
  (or sung) in 2 parts in an overlapping manner...the 2nd part starting
  after the 1st.

An interesting effect can be achieved with Rounds by having the 2nd
guitar(s) pick their strings close to the bridge. This produces a
sound much like a Harpsichord.

SHARPS AND FLATS

A sharp (♯) raises a note one fret
A flat (♭) lowers a note one fret

Between all natural notes a whole step apart, there exists another note. Each of these "in between" tones has two names. It can be called either the letter name of the lower note sharped, or that of the higher note flatted.

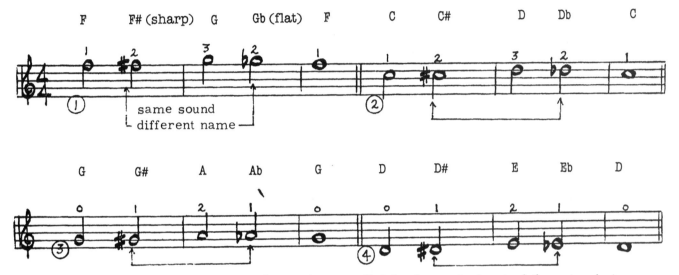

* In musical notation the symbol for sharp or flat is always in front of the note, but in speech, the word sharp (or flat) follows the letter name...therefore you say "F sharp, G flat, C sharp, etc..."

ABOUT THE GUITAR

IMPORTANT: On the guitar all notes A WHOLE STEP APART are TWO FRETS APART ...AND all notes A HALF STEP APART are ONE FRET APART

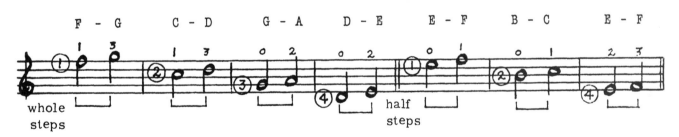

ALSO.. In the FIRST POSITION (where we are learning to play) from the last natural note on any string to the next natural note on the open string above, it is always a WHOLE STEP.

EIGHTH NOTES

Eighth notes receive half the time value of quarter notes... So eighth notes are played twice as fast as quarters. However, we will not move the pick any faster but, instead, make it more efficient by picking in both directions... Pick DOWN (Π) for notes falling ON the beat and pick UP (V) for those that occur OFF the beat.

Study

Remember: When playing 8th notes the picking direction matches that of the tapping foot... DOWN on the beat, and UP on notes counted "and."

Frere' Jacque

(ROUND)

25

CHORD STUDY

These C and G7th chords on the top 4 (and 5) strings will be needed in the next arrangement. The right hand may need some practice in strumming over 4 and 5 strings.

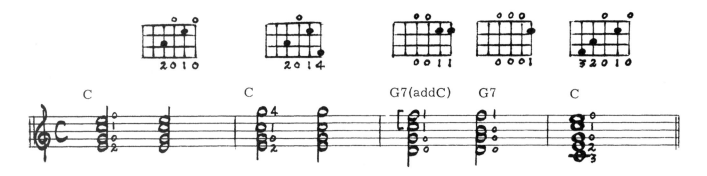

Rock Candy

W.G.L.

The student must learn all parts of all arrangements.

26

CHORD STUDY

Included in this study is the "tough" little F chord on the top strings...you'll have to keep after this one for quite a while to play it clearly.

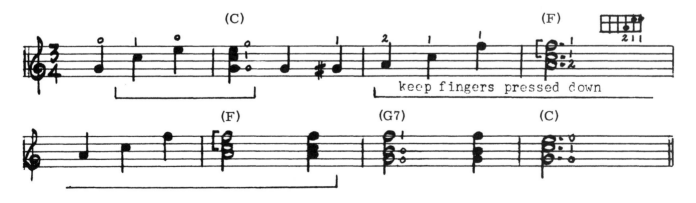

keep fingers pressed down

27

SHARPS AND FLATS

Remember: Sharped (#) notes are played one fret higher than natural notes....Flatted notes are played one fret lower than natural notes.

ON THE 1st STRING

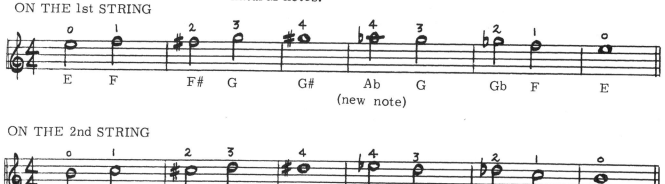

E   F   F#   G   G#   Ab   G   Gb   F   E

(new note)

ON THE 2nd STRING

B   C   C#   D   D#   Eb   D   Db   C   B

IMPORTANT: Once a sharp (or flat) appears in a measure, it applies to all notes with the same letter name that follow, until the bar line cancels it.

DOTTED QUARTER NOTES

Merrily We Roll Along

28

ABOUT SCALES

THE MAJOR SCALE is made up of 7 different notes (letter names) each a
whole step or a half step apart from each other according to the
following pattern....

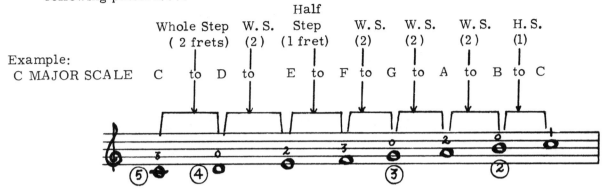

Example:
C MAJOR SCALE

MEMORIZE THIS SEQUENCE OF WHOLE AND HALF STEPS ⌐2+2+1⌐ +2 +⌐2+2+1⌐

Introduction of the NATURAL SIGN (♮)

The natural sign cancels out a sharp or flat. It is also
used as a "reminder" of the bar line cancellation.

STUDY WITH CHROMATICS   (Chromatics are raised or lowered notes instead of
the normal notes of the scale...)

* Remember the sharp (or flat) still applies until the bar line cancels it out.

Long, Long Ago

SHARPS AND FLATS

ON THE 3rd STRING

same note as
open 2nd string

ON THE 4tn STRING

(Be sure that you can name all natural and altered notes.)

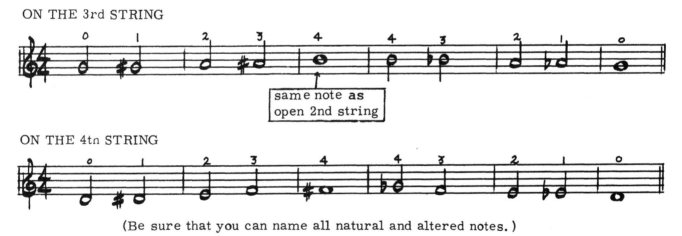

CHORD STUDY. . . . . This is important for strengthening the 1st and 3rd fingers

(Play again)

31

Home On The Range

This first note is called a "pick up" note. It is the 3rd beat of an imaginary
measure occurring before the actual beginning of the song.

Ritard poco a poco (get slower - little by little)

RITARD poco a poco

* This wavy line means to play a slower, more deliberate strum, so the notes of the chord will sound one after the other, in quick succession.

America The Beautiful

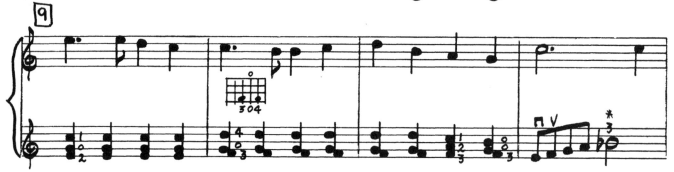

* Any sharp or flat that is added to the key in which you are playing
  is called an ACCIDENTAL. It applies only to (the remainder of) the
  measure in which it occurs.

The following new notes are an OCTAVE below those learned on page 4

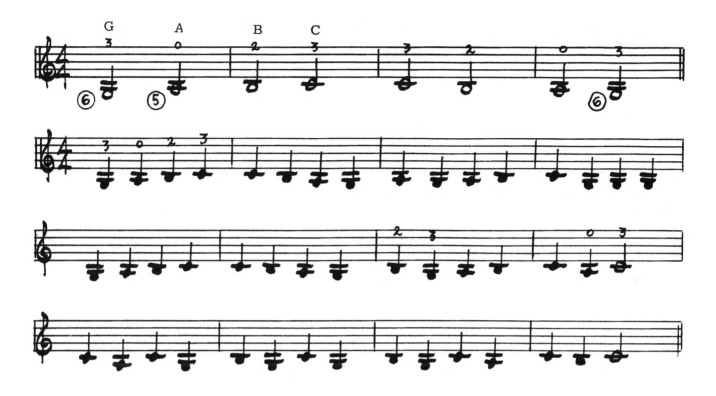

CHORD STUDY

The following C and F chords are played on the 3rd, 4th and 5th strings. To avoid striking too many strings use the next highest string (above those needed for the chord) as a pick stop. Push the pick right up against it... but not over it.

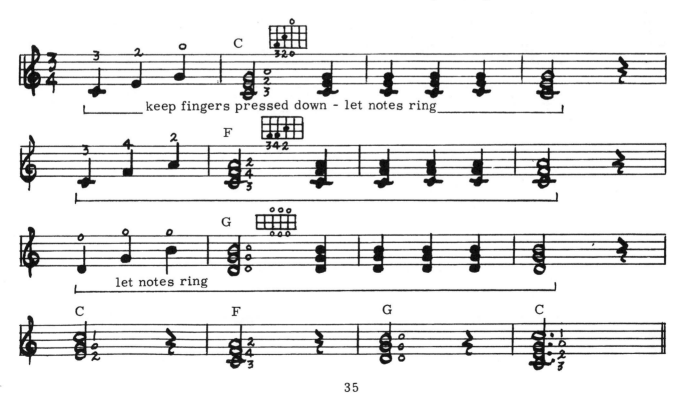

35

OCTAVES (See top of page 8)

Giant Steps

W.G.L.

THE C MAJOR SCALE .... extended to include the entire FIRST POSITION *

* THE FIRST POSITION on the guitar includes the 1st 4 frets, with the 1st
finger playing all notes occurring on the 1st fret, the 2nd finger the 2nd fret,
and so on. The first position is the only one that uses open strings extensively.

ASSIGNMENT......... write note names and insert bar lines. . (observe time signature). Play

ABOUT MAJOR SCALES   (2+2+1) +2+ (2+2+1)

A MAJOR SCALE can be built from any note, but because the sequence of whole and half steps must be followed exactly, we will have to use sharps (or flats) in them as part of the scale.

For example: TO BUILD A MAJOR SCALE FROM THE NOTE G

1. Write the 7 letter names or (notes) up from G and add another G (the octave) at the end.

2. Examine the intervals (whole and half steps). Notice that with these natural notes we have a half step between E and F where a whole step should occur. Also notice the whole step between F and the last G, which should be a half step.

3. We make these letter names (notes) conform to the sequence of whole and half steps necessary for a major scale, by merely sharping the F...which pushes this note a whole step away from E, and a half step closer to G.

If we start on F and build a major scale we find that with natural notes we have a whole step (instead of a half) between the 3rd and 4th notes, and only a half step (instead of a whole) between the 4th and 5th notes. To correct this we flat the note B...Therefore the scale or key of F MAJOR has all the B's flatted.

ASSIGNMENT . . . . Write the major scale (according to the sequence of whole and half steps) from the following notes.

> When sharps or flats are a necessary part of the scale they are written next to the clef sign at the beginning of each line of music (or stave). This eliminates the necessity of writing them again and again throughout the entire piece. The clef sign then, with or without sharps or flats next to it, becomes the scale indicator or KEY SIGNATURE.

The Cobra

(An Introduction to the MINOR Sound)

The following is a four part arrangement.   It is also playable with the first two or three parts.   The 4th part is to be played by laying the fingers of the left hand lightly across all of the strings to completely muffle them... DO NOT PRESS THEM DOWN.   Strike the muffled strings (like strumming chords) where indicated by the x's.   Other percussive sounds may be added to this rhythm part (such as snapping fingers, tapping with pencils, etc.)

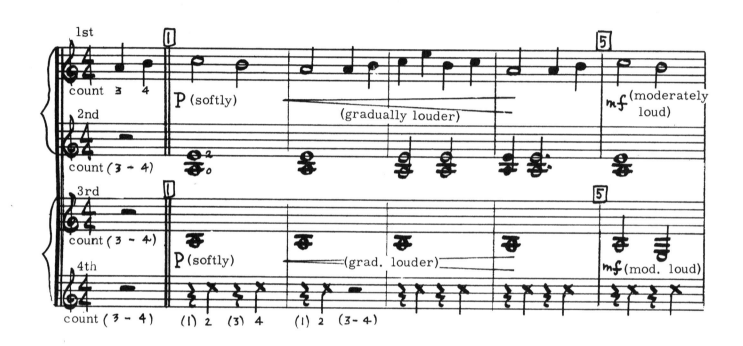

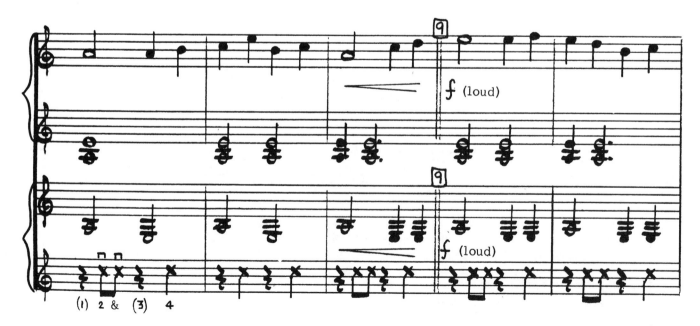

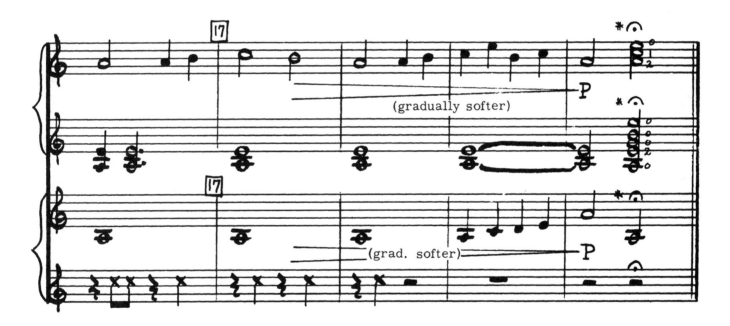

* This symbol is a FERMATA (fer-mah-tah)...it means "hold!")

When the words TOP or BOTTOM...HIGH or LOW...UP or DOWN are used in music they always refer to pitch (sound).
...The 1st or top string is the one with the highest sound..the bottom or 6th string is the one with the lowest sound.
...The higher notes (sounds) are played on the higher numbered frets..the lower notes are played on the lower numbered frets.
...Moving up the fingerboard means going toward the higher sounds (frets)..going down the fingerboard means moving toward the lower sounds (frets).

ALLA BREVE (CUT TIME)

There are two beats per measure in Alla Breve with the half note getting one count. All other time durations are reduced in the same ratio...(by one half). You could say that "CUT TIME" is twice as fast as four-four, or "COMMON TIME."

Duet For T.W.O.

W.G.L.

SYMBOL for Alla Breve (or Cut Time)

count 1 2 1 2

* For now, play all quarter notes, with down strokes of the pick...regardless of how they are counted in cut time.

40.

Bach Talk

(Excerpt from 2 part Invention No. 13)

J. S. Bach

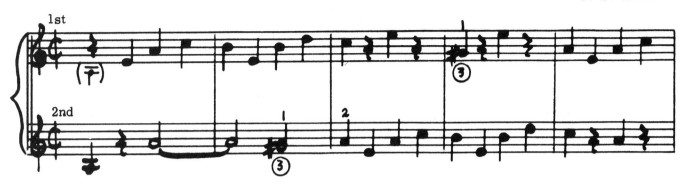

A VERY IMPORTANT CHORD STUDY

........The x found below the following diagrams means that these strings must be deadened and kept from sounding.   This is done by lightly touching (NOT PRESSING) the string with a part of the finger playing an adjacent string...(see below).

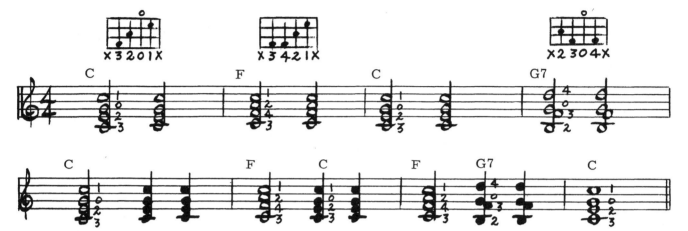

When playing chords it is often just as important to deaden certain strings as it is to press the proper ones.   This allows the right hand more freedom in strumming rhythms without accidentally sounding wrong notes on an open string.

The 1st string is easily deadened by lightly touching it with the fleshy part (or the side) of any finger playing the second string.

The 6th string is deadened by over-reaching, and touching with the tip of any finger playing the 5th string.   This is somewhat more difficult and therefore at times it is better for some players to reach around the neck with the thumb and lightly touch the 6th string to deaden it.

IMPORTANT.... strive to go from chord to chord without losing time or leaving large silences between them.

DILIGENT PRACTICE and patience are necessary to accomplish the above techniques.

SHARPS AND FLATS

ON THE 5th STRING

ON THE 6th STRING

THE EIGHTH NOTE REST . . . . It receives the same time value as an 8th note . . . one half beat in (Common Time).

Study

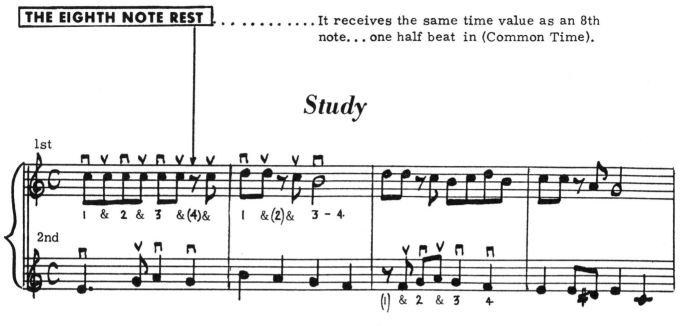

The Pebble

W.G.L.

43.

Accidentally

W. G. L.

44

* This wavy line means to play a slower, more deliberate strum so the
notes of the chord will sound one after the other, in quick succession.

(Note: in all 3 part arrangements the 3rd guitar part is optional)

45.

When a sharp (#) or flat (♭) is found in the key signature (between the G clef and the time signature) it applies to all notes with that letter name throughout the entire piece.

.... When the natural sign (♮) cancels a sharp (or flat) contained in the key signature it is an accidental and is therefore good only for the remainder of the measure in which it occurs.... The next bar line cancels the "natural" and the note again takes on the sharp or flat in the key signature.

THE G MAJOR SCALE . . . . . (All F's are sharped)

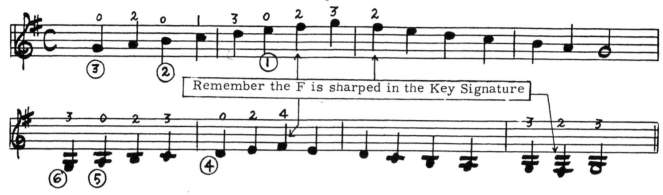

Remember the F is sharped in the Key Signature

Scale Study

1st

2nd

CHORD STUDY

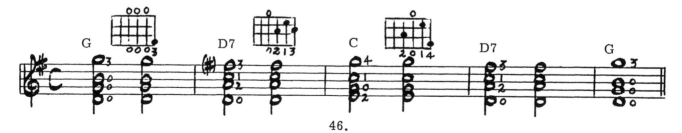

G   D7   C   D7   G

Lullabye

J. Brahms

47

My Old Kentucky Home

S. Foster

48

(*Remember the ♮ is still good until the bar line cancels it out...)

49.

Round

50

An Ancient Rock

W.G.L.

(* Observe all down strokes on chords as indicated for a stronger beat.)

CHORD BONUS

Dots represent finger placement. (Dots in parenthesis are optional notes)
Numbers below the diagram indicate fingers to be used. The 1st
   fingering below is usually the preferred one.
O (zero) is an open string.
X is a muted (silenced) string or one that must not be struck.

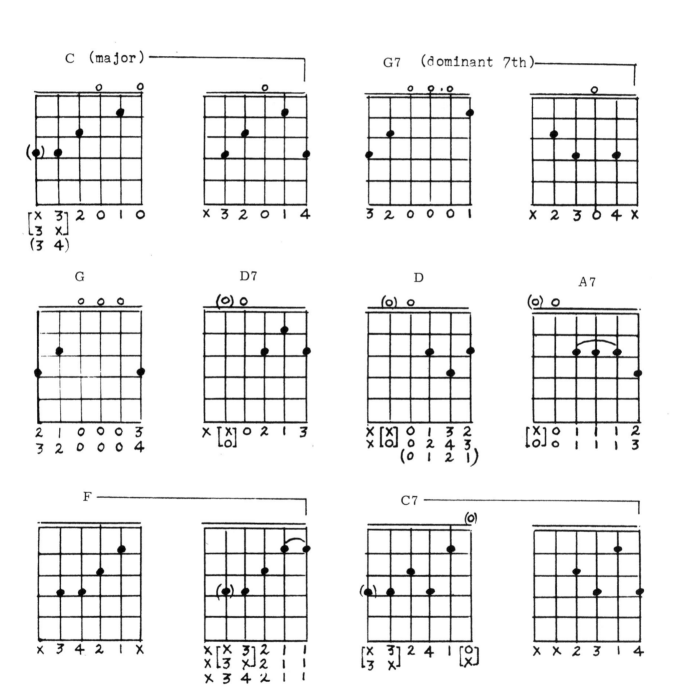

A
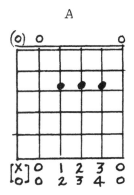
[X] 0 1 2 3 0
[O] 0 2 3 4 0

E7
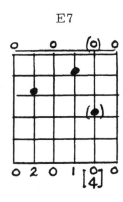
0 2 0 1 [O] 0
[4]

E
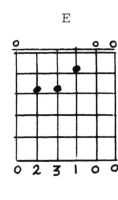
0 2 3 1 0 0

B7
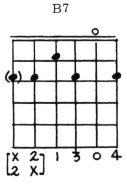
[X 2] 1 3 0 4
[2 X]

Em (minor)
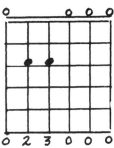

0 2 3 0 0 0

Am
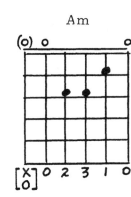
[X] 0 2 3 1 0
[O]

Dm
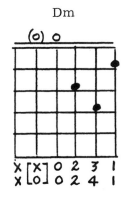
X [X] 0 2 3 1
X [O] 0 2 4 1

Gm
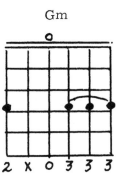
2 X 0 3 3 3

Fm
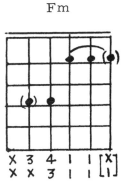
X 3 4 1 1 [X]
X X 3 1 1 [1]

DIMINISHED 7th CHORDS... (symbol is °)... 4 names for each chord
(Any note in the chord can be considered the ROOT or chord name)

C° A° Eb° F#°
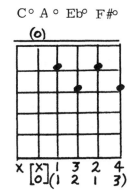
X [X] 1 3 2 4
[O] (1 2 1 3)

F° D° B° Ab°
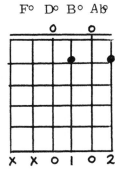
X X 0 1 0 2

E° G° Bb° C#°
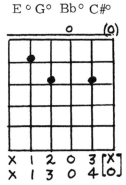
X 1 2 0 3 [X]
X 1 3 0 4 [O]

AUGMENTED CHORDS... (symbol is +) ... 3 names for each chord
(Any note in tne chord can be considered the ROOT or chord name)

G+ B+ Eb+
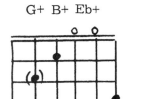
X [2] 1 0 0 4
[X]

D+ F#+ Bb+
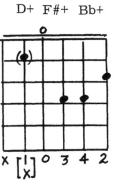
X [1] 0 3 4 2
[X]

F+ A+ C#+
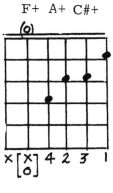
X [X] 4 2 3 1
[O]

C+ E+ Ab+
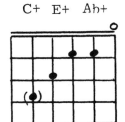
X X 3 1 2 0
(X 3 2 1 1 X)

CONCLUSION

Well, here we are (finally) at the end of this book. I sincerely hope you have had fun with the guitar and have been somewhat informed about music along the way.

If you are among those who have become intrigued with the instrument, and wish to embark on a more "in depth" study of it, I recommend delving into "THE MODERN METHOD FOR GUITAR" Volume One. With this Modern Method series I am attempting (to the best of my ability and experience) to aid the guitarist in his quest for a good working knowledge of the musical idiom and the never ending struggle for command of the instrument itself.

W.G.L.

Guitar Books and Videos
from Berklee Press

Berklee Press DVDs:
Just Press PLAY

Kenwood Dennard: The Studio/ Touring Drummer

ISBN: 0-87639-022-X	HL: 50448034	DVD $19.95

Up Close with Patti Austin: Auditioning and Making it in the Music Business

ISBN: 0-87639-041-6	HL: 50448031	DVD $19.95

The Ultimate Practice Guide for Vocalists

ISBN: 0-87639-035-1	HL: 50448017	DVD $19.95

Featuring Donna McElroy

Real-Life Career Guide for the Professional Musician

ISBN: 0-87639-031-9	HL: 50448013	DVD $19.95

Featuring David Rosenthal

Essential Rock Grooves for Bass

ISBN: 0-87639-037-8	HL: 50448019	DVD $19.95

Featuring Danny Morris

Jazz Guitar Techniques: Modal Voicings

ISBN: 0-87639-034-3	HL: 50448016	DVD $19.95

Featuring Rick Peckham

Jim Kelly's Guitar Workshop

ISBN: 0-634-00865-X	HL: 00320168	DVD $19.95

Basic Afro-Cuban Rhythms for Drum Set and Hand Percussion

ISBN: 0-87639-030-0	HL: 50448012	DVD $19.95

Featuring Ricardo Monzón

Vocal Technique: Developing Your Voice for Performance

ISBN: 0-87639-026-2	HL: 50448038	DVD $19.95

Featuring Anne Peckham

Preparing for Your Concert

ISBN: 0-87639-036-X	HL: 50448018	DVD $19.95

Featuring JoAnne Brackeen

Jazz Improvisation: Starting Out with Motivic Development

ISBN: 0-87639-032-7	HL: 50448014	DVD $19.95

Featuring Ed Tomassi

Chop Builder for Rock Guitar

ISBN: 0-87639-033-5	HL: 50448015	DVD $19.95

Featuring "Shred Lord" Joe Stump

Turntable Technique: The Art of the DJ

ISBN: 0-87639-038-6	HL: 50448025	DVD $24.95

Featuring Stephen Webber

Jazz Improvisation: A Personal Approach with Joe Lovano

ISBN: 0-87639-021-1	HL: 50448033	DVD $19.95

Harmonic Ear Training

ISBN: 0-87639-027-0	HL: 50448039	DVD $19.95

Featuring Roberta Radley